HISTORIC PHOTOS OF
GETTYSBURG

TEXT AND CAPTIONS BY JOHN S. SALMON

Turner®
Publishing Company
Nashville, Tennessee • Paducah, Kentucky

HISTORIC PHOTOS OF
GETTYSBURG

Turner Publishing Company
200 4th Avenue North • Suite 950   412 Broadway • P.O. Box 3101
Nashville, Tennessee 37219   Paducah, Kentucky 42002-3101
(615) 255-2665   (270) 443-0121

www.turnerpublishing.com

Historic Photos of Gettysburg

Copyright © 2007 Turner Publishing Company

Library of Congress Control Number: 2006937078

ISBN-10: 1-59652-323-9
ISBN-13: 978-1-59652-323-4

Printed in the United States of America

07 08 09 10 11 12 13 14—0 9 8 7 6 5 4 3 2 1

CONTENTS

ACKNOWLEDGMENTS VII

PREFACE VIII

THE BATTLE
    (1863) 1

DEDICATION AND REMEMBRANCE
    (1863–1900) 55

FIFTIETH REUNION
    (1913) 131

SEVENTY-FIFTH REUNION
    (1938) 171

NOTES ON THE PHOTOGRAPHS 200

BIBLIOGRAPHY 205

The North Carolina State Monument was dedicated on July 3, 1929. The sculptor, Gutzon Borglum, is most famous for his carving of the heads of presidents George Washington, Thomas Jefferson, Abraham Lincoln, and Theodore Roosevelt on Mount Rushmore in South Dakota. He was also the first sculptor to work on the massive monument to Confederate heroes at Stone Mountain, Georgia, although his work was obliterated after he had a falling out with the directors of the project and left the state. Augustus Lukeman finished the project.

Acknowledgments

This volume, *Historic Photos of Gettysburg,* is the result of the cooperation and efforts of many individuals, organizations, and corporations. It is with great thanks that we acknowledge the valuable contribution of the following for their generous support:

Gettysburg National Military Park Library
The Library of Congress
National Archives
Pennsylvania State Archives
U.S. Army Military Institute

We would also like to thank Emily J. and John S. Salmon for valuable contributions and assistance in making this work possible.

PREFACE

After stunning victories in Virginia early in May 1863 at Chancellorsville and Fredericksburg, Confederate general Robert E. Lee carried the war north, across the Mason-Dixon Line. His infantry marched through the Shenandoah Valley and central Maryland as Major General J. E. B. Stuart's cavalry harassed Union supply lines to the east. Union major general George G. Meade, who had replaced Major General Joseph Hooker as commander of the Army of the Potomac on June 28, led his force through Maryland and into Pennsylvania in pursuit. The Federals collided with Lee's Army of Northern Virginia at Gettysburg, Pennsylvania, on July 1, starting a battle neither side had intended to fight there. Three bloody days later, the defeated Confederates began retreating through Maryland to the Potomac River, where they crossed into Virginia on July 14.

This was Lee's second invasion of the North, the first having occurred in September 1862, which culminated in the Battle of Antietam on September 17. On that, the bloodiest single day in American history, about 23,000 men on both sides were killed, wounded, or reported missing. Mathew Brady, a noted New York and Washington portrait photographer, and his staff of outstanding cameramen were there to record the gruesome aftermath. For the first time, noncombatants far removed from the action saw what war really looked like when Brady later mounted an exhibition of his photographs. For generations reared on heroic, bloodless paintings and engravings, the images of mangled, bloated corpses were a shock. As a reporter for the *New York Times* wrote, "Mr. Brady has done something to bring to us the terrible reality and earnestness of the war. If he has not brought bodies and laid them in our door-yards and along [our] streets, he has done something very like it."

The historic photographs of Gettysburg, taken by Brady's men and others, make the reporter's words ring even more true, even to modern Americans who have grown to adulthood with images of war on the nightly news. That Civil War photographers accomplished so much with the massive equipment of the day, with wet glass plates developed in stifling darkroom wagons, makes those pioneer photojournalists seem almost superhuman. The images they created, which are preserved in the Library of Congress and elsewhere, constitute one of our nation's greatest historical treasures.

Turner Publishing Company is honored to issue this book, which contains some of the most important pictures taken just after the Battle of Gettysburg and during the years that followed. They depict not only the immediate effects of the battle, but also the ceremonies surrounding the Gettysburg Address, a statement of national purpose some historians consider the equal of the Declaration of Independence. They also show the veterans' reunions of 1913 and 1938, which have come to symbolize the reunification of the United States and the reconciliation of the soldiers who fought so bravely and so well on those July days in 1863. We salute their courage and steadfastness, and we encourage you to visit Gettysburg National Military Park to tread the ground they trod.

Todd Bottorff, Publisher

Mathew Brady took this view of Gettysburg from Seminary Ridge, northwest of the town, about July 15, 1863. Gettysburg was not the "sleepy village" of legend, but a bustling town and county seat located at the intersection of several main roads and turnpikes. It was the commercial hub of Adams County, and indeed of the surrounding region. On the afternoon of July 1, as Union and Confederate generals fed additional troops into the growing battle, Federal forces made a brief stand here before the Confederates swept them eastward to Cemetery Ridge.

THE BATTLE

(1863)

When Confederate general Robert E. Lee launched his second invasion of the North late in June 1863, he had several goals in mind. He intended to let his army live off the ripening farmlands of Maryland and Pennsylvania, threaten Northern cities to draw Union forces away from the South, encourage the Northern peace movement, and gain foreign recognition for the Confederacy. To accomplish the last goal—foreign recognition and perhaps even intervention—Lee wished to defeat a Federal army on its home soil.

Lee marched east through Pennsylvania, while Union major general George G. Meade, a native Pennsylvanian, led the Army of the Potomac northwest from Washington, D.C., to find the Confederates. Neither general knew where the other's army was located; each dispatched his cavalry to find out. Lee's infantry at first was far to the west of the Union cavalry, and Lee's cavalry, commanded by Major General J. E. B. Stuart, was far to the east of the Confederate commander and out of contact with him. Then, on July 1, a Confederate infantry brigade approached Gettysburg from the northwest, having heard that much-needed shoes could be obtained there. Just outside of town, it encountered two Union cavalry brigades. Soon Federal infantry arrived, and the unexpected and unplanned battle was joined. Under Confederate counterattacks, the Union infantry fell back, first to Seminary Ridge and then to Cemetery Ridge.

By the morning of July 2, the armies confronted each other across farm fields between the parallel ridges. The Union line, which faced west, stretched from Culp's Hill on the north, south along Cemetery Ridge, to Big Round Top and Little Round Top on the Federal left. The Confederates occupied Seminary Ridge, facing east. Between the opposing armies lay wheat fields, orchards, and the Emmitsburg Road. Lee launched unsuccessful attacks on the Union left flank at the southern end of Cemetery Ridge, and the carnage was great at Little Round Top and Devil's Den, and in the orchards and wheat fields. The day ended with another attack that failed, against Culp's Hill on the Federal right flank.

On the afternoon of July 3, after a ferocious artillery barrage that generally overshot its target, Lee launched an all-out assault on the center of Meade's line on Cemetery Hill. Famously if erroneously known as Pickett's Charge (Major General

George E. Pickett was but one of three division commanders leading the assault), this attack under the overall command of Major General James Longstreet foundered under Federal shot, shell, and small-arms fire. Lee began his retreat the next day, crossing the Potomac River into Virginia on July 14. His invasion had failed, at a cost of about 50,000 killed, wounded, and missing for the two sides.

Newspaper reporters described the action breathlessly, proclaiming that Gettysburg and "Pickett's Charge" constituted the "high-water mark" of the Confederacy. Historians continue to debate the battle's significance: whether Gettysburg or Antietam might better deserve to be called the war's turning point. Because of all that took place at Gettysburg, however—the carnage, the courage, the Charge, and the Address—there is no doubt that this is the ground most consecrated in American hearts.

This house, which was constructed about 1779 and belonged at the time of the battle to Mrs. Mary Thompson, served as Lee's headquarters because of its ideal location on the Chambersburg Turnpike at the crest of Seminary Ridge. Mrs. Thompson is standing beside her fence, on the right. Lee, as was his custom, slept in his tent, which was pitched at about the photographer's position. He and his staff used the Thompson house for meetings and meals. Brady took this picture on July 15.

Meade used this dwelling, the home of Mrs. Lydia A. Leister, as his headquarters after he arrived on the battlefield on July 2. This view, taken on July 6 before the Union army left Gettysburg, shows some of the damage—including dead horses—wrought by the Confederate artillery barrage just before the attack known as Pickett's Charge (actually the Pickett-Pettigrew-Trimble Charge) on July 3. Although the house was concealed from direct Confederate observation by high ground to the east of Cemetery Ridge, nothing could protect it from the bombardment. It was here that Meade decided on July 2 that the army would hold its ground, although he probably relocated his headquarters elsewhere once the shelling began.

Northwest of Gettysburg, as the fighting intensified during the afternoon of July 1, the Edward McPherson farm became the scene of combat. From the southeast, Union major general John F. Reynolds rushed his infantry to the support of the beleaguered cavalrymen, and soon arrived on the field himself. A Confederate sharpshooter's bullet struck his head as he rode elsewhere on the farm, and his horse carried him into nearby woods, where he died. McPherson's barn, shown here on the left and photographed by Brady about July 15, still stands. It was used as a hospital, and for some time was erroneously assumed to be the place where Reynolds died.

As in the preceding view taken about July 15, here Brady (on the right) is looking southeast at McPherson's Woods, with Seminary Ridge on the horizon. Brady's assistant is pointing to approximately the part of the woods where Reynolds died. The cupola of the Lutheran Seminary can be seen on the ridge to the left.

The ground here slopes up to the left, to Cemetery Ridge, in this view to the northwest from Stevens Knoll. Across this ground, from right to left, Colonel Isaac E. Avery led his North Carolina brigade against the Federals atop the ridge, during the afternoon of July 2. The 5th Maine Battery had been posted near the photographer's position, and the guns decimated the North Carolinians, who pressed on nonetheless until they were finally driven back. The picture was probably taken later in July, not long after the battle.

This view, facing northeast from the summit of Little Round Top to Cemetery Ridge in the distance, was recorded about July 15. It shows the center of the Federal position near Evergreen Cemetery. It also illustrates the significance of Little Round Top as the southern anchor of the Union line, for its command of the battlefield below.

In between Little Round Top and Big Round Top at the southern end of the Federal line on Cemetery Ridge, a collection of rocks and boulders later called Devil's Den formed a natural base for Southern sharpshooters, who captured the boulders on the afternoon of July 2. The Union troops on Little Round Top hastily constructed stone walls like this one, looking south to Big Round Top, to protect themselves.

These images, recorded on July 6, form a panorama looking from Devil's Den up to
Little Round Top as Confederate sharpshooters would have seen it.

The 102nd New York Infantry hastily erected and occupied these fieldworks on Culp's Hill on the evening of July 2. Five New York regiments defended the hill against Confederate attacks. Like most of the works, these were composed of stones, logs, and earth. Several of the trees around the men on the rocks in this photograph, taken about July 15, were still standing in the mid 1970s.

During the Civil War, the process by which photographs could be directly printed in newspapers and magazines had not been perfected. Publishers sometimes had engravers render line drawings from photographs, but there were advantages to using artists to paint or sketch scenes in the field instead. All the artists needed were paper and pencils or paints and brushes, whereas the photographers traveled with cumbersome equipment, chemicals, and fragile glass plates. One of the most noted combat artists, Alfred R. Waud, of *Harper's Weekly,* posed in Devil's Den on July 6 for photographer Timothy O'Sullivan.

Woods

Rebel batteries

Rebel battery

attack of Gen Hill & Longstreets got

Longstreets attack on the ... Thursday afternoon

2 Division 11 corps

2nd corps

3rd corps

... battery

Rocky Hill ... batteries

... corps

... western part of the battle

Road

Road

Rocky hill

... a sketch of the ...
... side
last night three

This army is moving very rapidly, ... It has been raining, almost continual...

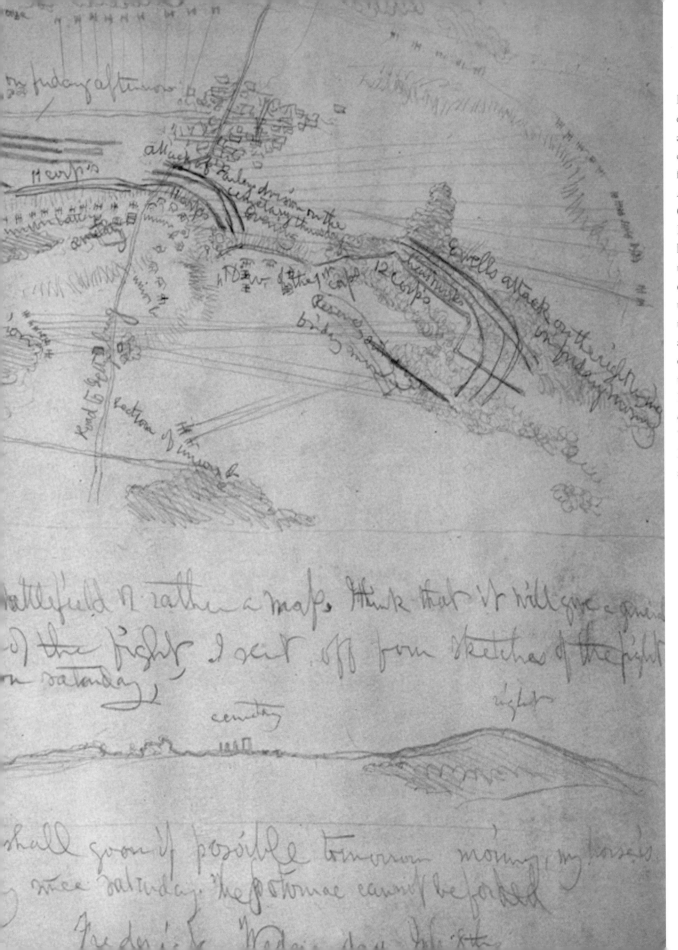

Edwin Forbes (1839–1895), one of the youngest combat artists of his time, drew camp and battlefield scenes for *Frank Leslie's Illustrated Newspaper* during the Civil War. Forbes was in Frederick, Maryland, when he made this sketch map of the Gettysburg battlefield on July 8, 1863. He was then accompanying part of the Army of the Potomac as it pursued the Army of Northern Virginia. At the top center of the map, Forbes noted the area of "Pickett's Charge" as "attack of Gen. Hill's and Longstreet's corps on friday afternoon."

Alexander Gardner, one of Brady's most talented photographers, took this view looking north from Little Round Top about July 15. The stone breastworks that the assistant is straddling are still in position on the Federal left flank. Today, the statue of Major General Gouvernor K. Warren, who recognized the importance of Little Round Top and ordered it secured only minutes before the Confederates attempted to occupy it on July 2, stands atop the boulder to the right of the pine tree.

This photograph taken from Cemetery Ridge near the Evergreen Cemetery gatehouse facing northwest shows the gun emplacements that Battery I, 1st New York Artillery, erected on July 2 to defend against Brigadier General Harry Hays's brigade, the Louisiana Tigers. Taken about July 9-11, this image shows Marie Tepe, known as French Mary, vivandiere of the 114th Pennsylvania Infantry. Vivandieres were officially attached to regiments to perform camp and nursing duties.

Brady photographed these Confederate prisoners posing on rail breastworks near the Lutheran Theological Seminary on Seminary Ridge about July 15, 1863. They are supposed to have been captured during the first day's fighting. According to notes with a copy of the image in the Library of Congress, the men are, from left to right, unidentified, Private Winborn L. Chafin, and Private W. H. Oliver, all of Hays's Louisiana Tigers. In fact, men named Winburn L. Chafin and W. M. Oliver served as privates in the 8th Louisiana Infantry, while William H. Oliver was a lieutenant in the regiment, according to the National Park Service's Civil War Soldiers and Sailors System (www.itd.nps.gov/cwss/).

18

"The Home of a Rebel Sharpshooter" was the title photographer James F. Gibson gave this image. In reality, the picture shows a dead Confederate infantryman—his slouch hat still on his head—at the edge of Devil's Den on the George W. Weikert farm. The soldier may have been killed on July 2 as Texas and Georgia Confederates attacked here. On the left, the neatly arranged wood may have been cut for a campfire. Gibson took the picture about July 6-7.

George J. White's stone house stood a few miles southwest of Gettysburg on the western side of Marsh Creek, not distant from the farthest right flank of the Confederate position on Seminary Ridge. The house, photographed in July 1863, appears on a postwar map with the notation that a nearby structure on the property was burned. The map shows a road leading southwest from Gettysburg and ending at the creek opposite the house, perhaps indicating that the creek was fordable there. Confederate troops and their Federal pursuers passed through the area after the battle and may have been responsible for burning the outbuilding. According to the 1860 census, White and his wife, Hester, lived in the house with their six children and one domestic servant, Barbara Eck.

This house was owned and occupied by Abram Bryan, a free black, on Cemetery Ridge a few hundred yards from Meade's headquarters. Brady photographed it about July 15, apparently under the impression that it and not the Leister house was the headquarters. Bryan and his family had fled the area in June when he learned that the Confederate army was approaching, perhaps fearing that they might be forced into slavery. Remodeled after the war, the house has since been returned to its appearance based on this and other photographs.

Mathew Brady photographed the Lutheran Theological Seminary about July 15, while it functioned as a hospital. During and after the battle, both sides used the building, which had been built in 1832, to treat the wounded. Each side also used its cupola as an observation post. Lee's headquarters was located nearby.

During the Confederate attack on Culp's Hill on the evening of July 2, sharpshooters supporting the assault used these boulders for cover. Combat artist Edwin Forbes made a painting of the scene, photographed here about July 15 from the Union perspective, that captured newspaper readers' attention.

The Zacharia Taney farmhouse near Spangler's Spring, with Rock Creek in the foreground, was in Confederate hands on the morning of July 3 and probably served as a hospital. The Confederate attack on Culp's Hill, the Federal right flank, failed, and Lee proceeded with plans for an assault on the Union center on Cemetery Ridge.

Mathew Brady and his assistants, some of whom appear here in the wagon at center, took several photographs of Little Round Top (left) and Big Round Top from the northwest on or about July 15.

Taken by Mathew Brady about July 15 looking west from Little Round Top, this image shows one of Brady's assistants, wearing his trademark broad-brimmed hat, in the foreground for scale. The George Rose farm is on the right beyond the first row of trees.

The Army of the Potomac under Major General George G. Meade had just left Gettysburg in pursuit of General Robert E. Lee's Army of Northern Virginia on July 7 when Timothy O'Sullivan took this photograph of Gettysburg from Cemetery Ridge. It offers a view of the town from the opposite direction of the preceding panorama, with the northern end of Seminary Ridge looming in the background. The tents on the right belong to a Pennsylvania militia regiment that had just arrived to occupy and guard Gettysburg after the battle, having marched along the Baltimore Turnpike in the foreground.

Timothy O'Sullivan took this picture of some of the Union dead on the battlefield, probably on the George Rose farm near Devil's Den, about July 5-6. Most of the photographs of dead soldiers made after the battle are of Confederates; this is one of only a handful taken of Federals. The mounted man in the background may be supervising a graves detail to bury the dead.

Alexander Gardner photographed these dead Confederate soldiers, probably Georgians or South Carolinians, who had been gathered for burial on the Rose farm, on July 5. Gardner's darkroom wagon is in the background.

The Union dead photographed here on the Rose farm on July 5 have been stripped of their shoes. It was common practice for soldiers, particularly the Confederates who sometimes lacked essentials like shoes, to relieve the dead of shoes and other articles that the living needed.

On July 6, Timothy O'Sullivan, working with Alexander Gardner, photographed this unidentified Confederate soldier he found lying in Devil's Den. This image shows the young man's body in the position in which it was found.

O'Sullivan and his assistants then moved the body of the Confederate "sharpshooter" to this position in Devil's Den, where soldiers earlier had built a stone wall between the boulders for protection. The photographer added the weapon as a prop to simulate a sniper's nest and thus created one of the best-known photographs made on the Gettysburg battlefield.

Devil's Den, photographed by Peter S. Weaver on November 11, was the scene of intense combat on July 2. The Confederates attacked the Union left flank here from Seminary Ridge, seen faintly as a row of trees in the background on the left of the picture. Elements of the 4th Maine Infantry defended this position against assaults by Alabama and Georgia infantry regiments.

The Confederates who attacked the Federal position at Devil's Den on July 2 came across the ground shown here at the base of Big Round Top. So many of them were cut down that the area was named the Slaughter Pen after Timothy O'Sullivan photographed it on July 6. The dead Confederates, strewn among the boulders, were buried soon after this image was made.

This unfinished Confederate grave likely was dug at the Rose farm near the peach orchard there. The single headboards, typical of Confederate burials, suggest that these men may have died of their wounds in the Rose house, which was used as a hospital after the fighting on July 2. Their comrades then began to bury them but were unable to finish the task before the next day's combat called them away. Timothy O'Sullivan took this photograph on July 5.

During the Confederate attack on the Union left flank on July 2, Captain John Bigelow's battery, 9th Massachusetts Artillery, was stationed on the Abraham Trostle farm, near the house and barn. Confederate brigadier general William Barksdale's Mississippi infantry brigade assaulted Bigelow's position, pushing the artillerists from their position and capturing four of Bigelow's six cannons, probably by shooting the artillery horses to prevent the pieces from being removed. About fifty horses were killed around the barn and the house, and were still lying in place when Timothy O'Sullivan made this photograph on July 6.

Alexander Gardner's photographers documented six dead Confederate soldiers at the foot of Big Round Top from several angles on July 6. Although the exact position has not been identified, it appears to have been in or near the Slaughter Pen. After the fighting, on July 2, the Federals abandoned Devil's Den nearby and the Confederates took it over.

Undoubtedly the most gruesome of all the photographs taken at Gettysburg, this image was thought for many years (because of the original caption) to depict a Confederate killed by an artillery shell on July 2. One such shell lies conveniently on the ground beyond the soldier's right knee, as if in support of the supposition. His dismembered hand is visible in front of the carefully positioned rifle. Rather than an artillery shell, it is far more likely that a bullet felled the soldier, probably a Georgian, in the farm field adjoining Rose Woods, where his body was then mutilated by wandering hogs. Alexander Gardner made the photograph on July 5.

Originally titled "Unfit for Service," this photograph of a dead artillery horse and its limber was taken on July 6 by Alexander Gardner. About 1,500 artillery horses were killed during the three-day battle and lay moldering in the summer heat and humidity for weeks thereafter. The limber, which served a "Light 12 P[ounde]r Gun," has spilled its contents—shot, shell, and other artillery equipment—on the ground. The exact site of this picture is not known.

Because of the heat and humidity of the Pennsylvania summer, most of the soldiers killed in the battle were quickly gathered and buried. Very soon thereafter, curious Northerners began coming to the battlefield, joining those who were there to search for loved ones among the dead and wounded. Some photographers posed live soldiers as dead ones, as in this image, one of several that Peter S. Weaver took at Devil's Den on November 11 looking toward Little Round Top. Such images fed the growing public fascination with the battle.

Evergreen Cemetery, located atop Cemetery Ridge, was established in 1853, and the handsome gatehouse was constructed two years later. Timothy O'Sullivan took this picture late in the morning of July 7, just after the last units of the Union army had set off in pursuit of the retreating Confederates. The earthworks in the foreground, remnants of which are visible today, protected the guns of Battery B, 4th U.S. Artillery, during the battle. The image is notable for the inclusion of the carriage, whose occupants were among the first civilians to tour the battlefield.

It is not known whether this amputation scene at Camp Letterman Hospital was real or staged, but it was probably the latter. The photograph probably was taken in October 1863. The men who died of their wounds, or of the treatments—such as amputation—for their wounds, were buried in the hospital cemetery.

On the morning of November 19, 1863, a large crowd and many dignitaries processed to the new Soldiers' National·Cemetery on Cemetery Ridge for the dedication ceremony. Among the latter were Secretary of War William H. Seward, Postmaster General Montgomery C. Blair, and President Abraham Lincoln, who rode a "chestnut bay horse," according to a witness. Lincoln's "towering figure surmounted by a high silk hat made the rest of us look small." This photograph, made looking northward on Baltimore Street from the intersection with Emmitsburg Road, shows the procession turning right on its way to the cemetery.

Eastern Cemetery Hill is seen from Stevens Knoll in this photograph, taken in 1889. Confederate forces attacked from right to left across the open ground on July 2, 1863, but the Federals repulsed the assault. On the hill in the background stands the observation tower erected in 1878 and dismantled in 1895.

John L. Burns, a nearly seventy-year-old resident of Gettysburg, lived in a house that no longer stands just south of the Chambersburg Turnpike at the western edge of town. On July 1, 1863, he heard the sounds of combat to the northwest and no doubt learned what was happening from Union soldiers hastening past his door to the fight. During a noontime lull in the action, he picked up his ancient flintlock rifle and some ammunition and walked to the McPherson farm, where he fought alongside the young soldiers of the 150th Pennsylvania Infantry, the only civilian to engage in combat during the battle. Burns, wounded three times, became a local hero, and President Abraham Lincoln asked to meet him during his visit to Gettysburg in November that year.

Owned and operated by Samuel Fahnestock, this clothing store was one of the largest commercial buildings in Gettysburg in 1863, when Alexander Gardner photographed it about July 9. The store stood on Baltimore Street; the current structure there incorporates the building but has been much altered. Here, on July 1, 1863, Union major general Oliver O. Howard stood on the flat roof and observed the opening phase of the battle northwest of town. After the battle, the store became the new headquarters of the U.S. Sanitary Commission, a civilian organization that hired physicians to examine camps and recommend improvements in hygiene, augmented dull rations with healthier food, collected and distributed medical supplies, and gave relief to sick and needy soldiers. The commission moved its offices to Camp Letterman Hospital later in July.

Because of the enormous number of wounded Union soldiers and captured Confederates—about 22,000—the Federals established tent hospitals immediately after the battle, and transferred to them the casualties lying in the houses, barns, and other buildings that served as temporary field hospitals during the fighting. This is one of the few photographs taken of a tent hospital in July; it belonged to the Union II Corps.

About mid July, as life began to return to a semblance of normalcy in Gettysburg, the U.S. Army established Camp Letterman General Hospital and transferred the wounded there from the various other tent hospitals. The new hospital was located on the George Wolf farm about a mile and a half east of town on the York Turnpike, on a well-drained hill with a good spring for water. It was a healthy place to treat the soldiers until they were well enough to travel to the hospitals in Philadelphia, Baltimore, and other cities. The tent with a wreath at its apex and the U.S. flag in the background sheltered the U.S. Sanitary Commission at Camp Letterman Hospital, probably photographed in October or November 1863.

This photograph shows the kitchen at Camp Letterman General Hospital in the autumn of 1863.

While Camp Letterman Hospital operated, the Sanitary Commission did much to alleviate the suffering of the wounded soldiers. The group of men and women in this picture made in August 1863 include commission superintendent Gordon Winslow (seated, with a white beard), with Mrs. Winslow standing at the left of the table, Surgeon Chamberlain (sitting on the table), and Mrs. Sampson (seated to the left of Superintendent Winslow). By November 10, only about a hundred patients remained at Camp Letterman Hospital, which closed a few weeks later. George Wolf got his farm back, and soon only the graveyard remained to indicate that the hospital had been there. Confederate remains were exhumed in 1872 and 1873 for relocation to Southern cemeteries. The Union dead were removed in 1864 to the new burial ground on Cemetery Ridge. It was called Soldiers' National Cemetery, and it was dedicated late in November 1863 in a ceremony that would be long remembered.

Dedication and Remembrance

(1863–1900)

Soon after the Battle of Gettysburg, a military cemetery was established adjoining the private Evergreen Cemetery atop Cemetery Ridge. About 3,500 Union dead were eventually transferred there from numerous battlefield and hospital burial sites. On November 19, a dedication ceremony was held to open the new cemetery. Although the principal speaker was Edward Everett, one of the most famous orators of the day, officials also invited the president, Abraham Lincoln, to make "a few appropriate remarks." Lincoln arrived in Gettysburg by train the day before the ceremony and spent the night at the home of David Wills. The next morning, Lincoln and other dignitaries rode in a procession to the new Soldiers' National Cemetery for the dedication ceremony. Everett's eloquent two-hour oration has long since been forgotten. Lincoln's remarks, delivered in two minutes, have become immortal.

The Gettysburg battlefield, like several others, soon became a tourist destination. Within days of the battle, family members came searching for loved ones in the hospitals and temporary gravesites. Local residents rode and walked across fields and through woods to view the damage the battle had wrought to their own and their neighbors' farms. Survivors of the fight marked sites of significance to them with paint and wood. For example, the tree under which Major General John F. Reynolds died was soon identified by the letter *R* painted on it. Even before war's end, efforts were underway to preserve not only single sites but also larger portions of the battlefield. Photographers followed in the wake of Mathew Brady, Alexander Gardner, and Timothy O'Sullivan, taking pictures of famous locations and offering them for sale to a seemingly insatiable public as stereopticon views and postcards.

Local citizens established the Gettysburg Battlefield Memorial Association in 1864 to protect some of the land as a memorial to the Union soldiers who had fought there. In succeeding years, so much land was acquired that in 1895, the federal government accepted custody and established Gettysburg National Military Park. A commission of Civil War veterans administered the park and coordinated the placement of markers to identify the battle lines and memorialize regiments and generals. In 1933, the National Park Service began to administer the park, and to preserve and interpret the Battle of Gettysburg and the Gettysburg Address to visitors.

About 3,000 people attended the Soldiers' National Cemetery dedication ceremony. This image was taken from the edge of the crowd looking generally east toward the speakers' platform, which is indicated by the slight rise on the horizon between the Evergreen Cemetery gatehouse on the left and the large tent on the right.

The exact site of the speakers' platform from which Lincoln delivered his Address has been the subject of some disagreement over the years. This monument, the Soldiers' National Monument completed in the National Cemetery in 1869, was long claimed to mark the spot. Now, however, the platform is believed to have been within the bounds of Evergreen Cemetery, not far from the monument.

To support the troops taking part in the ceremonies for the laying of the cornerstone for the Soldiers' National Monument, food and other supplies were collected and distributed. This photograph, taken by Alexander Gardner in July 1865, shows the camp of Captain John J. Hoff, commissary of subsistence, U.S. Volunteers. Hoff himself is lounging against the tent pole on the right.

Following Spread: By July 1865, when photographer William Morris Smith made this image, a small gatehouse had been erected at the entrance to the Soldiers' National Cemetery.

On the hill in the background near the gatehouse can be seen the guns and men of the Horse Artillery Brigade of the Army of the Potomac, as well as of Battery A, 4th U.S. Artillery. Captain James M. Robertson, who had led the 1st Horse Artillery Brigade during the battle, commanded them. In the foreground, soldiers of the 50th Pennsylvania Infantry have stacked their weapons amid the graves, which are marked by upright boards, in the Soldiers' National Cemetery. The occasion, on July 4, 1865, was the laying of the cornerstone for the Soldiers' National Monument.

William Morris Smith photographed Captain John J. Hoff's unnamed clerk, looking as if he were attending to business, seated on a rock beside Hoff's tent.

Probably taken behind Hoff's tent, this image shows Hoff second from the right. He employed the African American men, in civilian clothing, as cooks.

The officers of the 50th Pennsylvania Infantry, commanded by Colonel William H. Telford, posed for William Morris Smith at what appears to be an artillery emplacement at Gettysburg about July 4, 1865.

George Smyser, a prominent Gettysburg banker, died on October 3, 1857, and was buried in Evergreen Cemetery. His monument, the obelisk depicted here in 1865, was erected soon after his death, and was therefore in place during the Battle of Gettysburg. C. J. Tyson took this photograph facing northeast.

Telford and his officers posed again, probably for Alexander Gardner, at their camp in the woods at the foot of Culp's Hill, about July 4, 1865. This time a local hero joined them. John Burns, the civilian who left his house in Gettysburg to fight in the first day's battle, is seated at far left in the front row.

The entire 50th Pennsylvania Infantry regiment stood in formation at its camp on the edge of the woods at the foot of Culp's Hill when Alexander Gardner photographed the unit about July 4, 1865.

71

William Morris Smith photographed Colonel William Davis and the staff officers of the 69th Pennsylvania Infantry at Gettysburg in June 1865. The regiment, which may have been present for the laying of the Soldiers' National Monument cornerstone, had played a key role in repulsing the Pickett-Pettigrew-Trimble Charge at the Bloody Angle on July 3, 1863.

The commemoration of key events and important individuals in the Battle of Gettysburg began soon after the fighting ended. This is one of several trees on the edge of McPherson's Woods alleged to mark the site of the death of Union major general John F. Reynolds on July 1, 1863, the first day of the battle. The dark mark on the trunk just above the temporary grave marker leaning against the tree is the letter *R*. The grave marker, which photographer C. J. Tyson probably moved to this position when he recorded the image about 1867, is inscribed with the name Williams. The remains of W. Williams, Company B, 24th Michigan Cavalry, were removed from the battlefield to the Soldiers' National Cemetery during the winter of 1863–1864. Williams's regiment suffered severe losses in the area of McPherson's Woods during the battle.

Several postwar photographs exist of the Lutheran Theological Seminary, a handsome building constructed in 1832. This one, a Tipton and Myers view captioned "Theological Seminary, used as a hospital during and after the battle," may have been taken about 1868.

Posing among trees damaged by the fighting for Culp's Hill on the morning of July 3, 1863, three Union veterans return to "the woods where the 147 [147th Pennsylvania Infantry] lay at the time of the charge of the rebels on Culps Hill near Spanglers Lane." The photograph, according to the caption, was "taken from the lane looking southeast." Today, a regimental monument stands near the spot.

This battlefield observation tower on Cemetery Ridge was photographed about 1878. George Arnold, one of the directors of the Gettysburg Battlefield Memorial Association, erected it in the spring of that year. It was demolished in August 1895 to make room for the Major General Winfield S. Hancock equestrian statue. At the time the tower was built, it was a widely applauded addition to the battlefield. A century later, however, another tower, constructed in 1974 just outside Gettysburg National Military Park, came to be regarded as a blot on the landscape and was demolished in 2000.

During the years following the end of the war, individuals and groups of former soldiers went to the Gettysburg battlefield to see again the places where they had fought. Soon, organizations such as the Grand Army of the Republic, the Union veterans' organization, began to hold conventions and reunions there. This G.A.R. camp was photographed in 1878 at its first annual reunion.

This Grand Army of the Republic encampment was held in 1880.
Parades and reenactments of parts of the battle were among the activities.

The Nicholas Codori farm was located in the route of the Confederate attack on Cemetery Hill on July 3, 1863—the assault popularly known as Pickett's Charge. The Codori house and other buildings, including the barn pictured here, broke up the advance of parts of Major General George E. Pickett's division as the men maneuvered around the structures. This photograph was made in 1882; the barn was replaced two years later.

Former Union cavalrymen pose at the dedication of the Gregg Cavalry Shaft at Gettysburg on October 15, 1884. The seated men include Colonel William Brooke Rawle (second from left), Brigadier General David McM. Gregg (fourth from left), and Brigadier General John I. Gregg (fifth from left). David Gregg, who fought Confederate Major General J. E. B. Stuart's cavalry here, was known as one of the best cavalry officers in the U.S. Army. The column is named in his honor.

During the fight for Little Round Top on July 2, 1863, a Confederate bullet struck Acting Brigadier General Stephen H. Weed in the spine, paralyzing him below the shoulders. Carried to the relative safety of a large boulder, Weed said, "I'm as dead a man as Julius Caesar." He died a short time later, and after the war this monument was erected in his memory. The photograph, taken in 1883, shows little development on the site except for the monument.

This view shows the terrain from the Weed Monument on Little Round Top to Devil's Den and the battlefield beyond.

This photograph, also taken from Little Round Top but from a position farther to the right than the previous images, shows some of the ground covered by the Pickett-Pettigrew-Trimble Charge. The picture was taken in September 1885.

This image of the area of the Pickett-Pettigrew-Trimble Charge was photographed from behind a stone wall on the Codori farm in 1885. For all its subsequent fame, the "Pickett's Charge" site was not photographed at first as extensively as other sites.

In September 1885, a photographer captured this view of Gettysburg from Cemetery Ridge.

Now known as Jennie Wade, Mary Virginia Wade actually spelled her nickname *Ginnie*. She gained posthumous fame as the only civilian killed during the Battle of Gettysburg. A stray Confederate bullet tore through two doors before striking her in the back on the morning of July 3, 1863, as she baked bread in this house, the home of her sister, Georgia Anna Wade McClellan, who had recently given birth. The undated postcard depicts Jennie Wade, the house in which she was killed, and her monument.

Delegations from Massachusetts regiments pose at Gettysburg in front of the 2nd Massachusetts Infantry monument in 1885. This monument, erected in 1879, is considered the first substantial memorial to be erected on the battlefield, after a small marker was put up on Little Round Top on August 1, 1878, to mark the spot where Colonel Strong Vincent fell. The Massachusetts marker stands at Spangler's Meadow, where the regiment briefly held the Confederate tree line after a charge, on July 2, 1863.

On June 21, 1888, veterans of the 96th Pennsylvania Infantry gather at Gettysburg for the dedication of their regimental monument. Major William S. Lessig led the regiment on July 2, 1863, as it defended its ground near Little Round Top.

Veterans of the 151st Regiment, Pennsylvania Volunteer Infantry, gather for the dedication of their regimental monument on July 1, 1888. The monument marks the site near McPherson's Woods where, on July 1, 1863, the regiment rushed to fill a gap in the Union line that the 26th North Carolina Infantry was about to exploit.

On July 2, 1863, Major General Daniel E. Sickles, commanding the Union III Corps, violated orders and moved his corps forward of the rest of the Federal line, creating a bulge or salient vulnerable to Confederate attack. Confederate Major General James Longstreet attacked the salient late in the afternoon, inflicting heavy casualties, particularly on Union soldiers in the area of a wheat field and Joseph Sherfy's peach orchard. The 9th Massachusetts Battery, whose monument is depicted here, was the last Federal artillery battery to withdraw from the peach orchard to Little Round Top.

Union breastworks still stood on Culp's Hill in this undated late-nineteenth-century photograph.

This photograph shows the 12th New York Infantry monument near Devil's Den, surmounted by a statue of Colonel Augustus van Horne Ellis, the regiment's commander. Ellis fell while leading a charge here on July 2, 1863.

Taken at a gathering of the Military Order of the Loyal Legion of the United States, this image shows "Bugler Henry standing at Warren Statue, Little Round Top, April 18th, 1890." The Loyal Legion was founded in Philadelphia in the wake of President Abraham Lincoln's assassination, and its members pledged to protect the national government from similar threats. It is now a hereditary organization whose members are descended from Civil War officers on the Union side.

This "Group of Ladies" pose with a cannon, which is displayed at the "clump of trees" during the Loyal Legion gathering in April 1890.

One of the many groups of veterans who returned to the battlefield is depicted in this undated image.

Captain Joseph M. Knap recruited men from the Pittsburgh area for his independent battery at the start of the war. Attached to the 28th Pennsylvania Infantry, the battery fought in Virginia in the Shenandoah Valley, as well as at Cedar Mountain, Antietam, Chancellorsville, Gettysburg, and in Georgia. During the Battle of Gettysburg, on July 2, 1863, three guns were posted on the summit of Culp's Hill, from which they engaged Confederate artillery on another hill nearby; Knap's guns silenced the Confederate cannons. This photograph was taken at a reunion of Knap's Battery in the field below Culp's Hill.

This undated view of Gettysburg shows the old dormitory of
Pennsylvania College (now Gettysburg College) on the far left.

The monument to Major General John F. Reynolds, which stands in the Soldiers' National Cemetery, was erected in 1871. It was the first sculptural monument to an individual to be placed on the battlefield.

In this undated photograph, a veteran has brought his wife to the battlefield to show her where he fought. According to the caption, "the gentleman in the picture is a member of the 2nd Mass. Regiment, the lady his wife. They were visiting the spot and sat at the spring [Spangler's Spring] to rest when this was taken."

A visitor to Devil's Den ponders life and death amongst the boulders in this undated photograph.

These three men in Devil's Den are probably veterans, whose numbers
began to dwindle rapidly late in the nineteenth century.

Major General Daniel E. Sickles (center), poses with Brigadier General Charles K. Graham (left) and Brigadier General Joseph B. Carr (right), on a visit to Gettysburg, perhaps in 1893. The men are standing near the Trostle barn, on or about the spot where Sickles was wounded. He lost his leg, gave the shattered bone to the medical museum of the Library of Congress, and paid it sentimental visits periodically. He headed the New York State Monument Commission to oversee the erection of monuments at Gettysburg. In 1893, after he was elected a congressman from New York, he led the effort to establish Gettysburg National Military Park. Sickles ultimately prevailed two years later.

When Congress created the Gettysburg National Military Park in 1895, it assigned the administration of the park to the War Department. Since the department focused on instruction and the military use of its landholdings, the needs of tourists took second place to the needs of the army. The men in this group, posed around the Warren statue on Little Round Top, are army officers from Fort Leavenworth, Kansas, on a "staff ride." The staff ride, which is still employed today, is a way to instruct young officers in military tactics by visiting important battlefields such as Gettysburg. The National Park Service assumed the administration of the park in 1933.

The equestrian statue of Major General Winfield Scott Hancock,
located on East Cemetery Hill, was dedicated on June 5, 1896.
This image was probably made not long thereafter.

After Gettysburg National Military Park was established in 1895, the commissioners in charge set about making significant improvements to the infrastructure, especially to the roads. Tourists such as those depicted here found it easier to drive through the park in their cars. The monument is that of the 155th Pennsylvania Infantry (Pittsburgh Zouaves), located on Little Round Top.

A group of veterans attending a reunion pose beside the monument to the 68th Pennsylvania Infantry on the Emmitsburg Road at Sherfy's peach orchard late in the nineteenth century.

The gatehouse to Evergreen Cemetery was probably photographed after the national park was created. The cannon in the foreground marks the position of Stewart's Battery B, 4th U.S. Artillery, during the battle.

This monument to Brigadier General Samuel K. Zook, who was mortally wounded leading his brigade in a charge across the wheat field on July 2, 1863, was erected in 1882.

Recorded about 1900, this view of the Soldiers' National Cemetery extends from the Major General John F. Reynolds monument in the foreground to the Soldiers' National Monument in the rear.

Taken from the observation tower on Cemetery Ridge, this photograph faces roughly south along the ridge to the Round Tops. The Bloody Angle is visible in the center of the image to the right of the road, as well as a number of Union monuments. This was the focus of "Pickett's Charge" on July 3, 1863.

Visitors examine the headstones in the Soldiers' National Cemetery, with the Soldiers' National Monument in background on the right, about 1903. The New York State Monument, dedicated on July 2, 1893, is to the left.

The legendary Spangler's Spring, where Union and Confederate soldiers supposedly called a truce for water on the night of July 2, 1863, has been covered with various springhouses over the years. These men and boys were photographed there about 1903.

This photograph shows a military encampment at Gettysburg about 1909. It may have been erected for the dedication of the U.S. Regulars Monument and the visit of President William Howard Taft. In the distance on the left, a blimp or tethered balloon, perhaps intended to carry photographers aloft, lies on the ground.

The area of the second day of the Battle of Gettysburg is seen here facing northwest from Little Round Top. The picture was taken about 1909.

This panorama, made about 1909, shows the site of the third day's battle and Meade's headquarters, to the left.

On the summit of Barlow's Knoll, scene of the fighting on July 1, 1863, stand the 17th Connecticut Infantry monument and cannons in this 1909 photograph.

The 1st Massachusetts Infantry monument, located on the
Emmitsburg Road in the field of the Pickett-Pettigrew-Trimble
Charge, was dedicated in 1913.

Taken on the Chambersburg Turnpike, this image illustrates the extent to which the generals and regiments that had taken part in the great battle of 1863 had been memorialized by 1909, when this photograph was taken. On the left side of the turnpike, from left to right, the monuments are those of Major General John Buford, Battery B, 2nd Maine Artillery, and Major General John F. Reynolds.

Those Union and Confederate veterans who returned to Gettysburg in 1913 for the first time since the battle were no doubt astonished at the changes that had occurred. They would have expected to see most of the battleground returned to the uses it had before the clash, and the growth of the town would not have surprised them. But to find the place so parklike, and covered with monuments, must have been strange indeed. This photograph of the well-groomed Soldiers' National Cemetery shows the New York State Monument and neatly arranged flags at each gravesite.

FIFTIETH REUNION

(1913)

In 1908, former Union lieutenant colonel Henry S. Huidekoper, 150th Pennsylvania Infantry, called on Pennsylvania governor Edwin Stuart to suggest that an observance be held at Gettysburg in 1913 to mark the fiftieth anniversary of the battle. Stuart agreed, and a year later the state assembly established and funded a commission to plan the commemoration. Several other states also established boards to help. In 1910, the U.S. Congress created a federal commission to coordinate with Pennsylvania. Momentum and support for the commemoration grew as the anniversary approached, even in the southern states. The president general of the United Daughters of the Confederacy urged the organization's chapters to raise funds to send Confederate veterans to the reunion. The state of Pennsylvania promised to take care of transporting all veterans within the state's borders, but the former soldiers had to get that far on their own.

All honorably discharged veterans were invited to attend. The two main veterans' groups, the Grand Army of the Republic and the United Confederate Veterans, encouraged their members to take part. In all, 44,713 Union veterans and 8,694 Confederate veterans attended. Every state had at least one representative at Gettysburg. Two governors were present who had served in the Confederate army: William Hodges Mann of Virginia and James B. McCreary of Kentucky. Major General Daniel E. Sickles, who had commanded a Union corps, was there, as was the senior surviving Confederate major general, Evander K. Law. The youngest veteran in attendance was reported to be sixty-one years old, while the oldest claimed to be one hundred and twelve. An enormous city of tents housed the veterans and provided them with food, medical care, and as many of the comforts of home as could be supplied.

The reunion and commemoration ceremonies took place over four days. Speeches of welcome dominated July 1, 1913, designated Veterans' Day. On July 2, in the Great Tent that sheltered thousands of people, veterans gave their own addresses and Barry Bulkley read the Gettysburg Address. Bulkley's father, John Wells Bulkley, had been the first physician to minister to Abraham Lincoln after the president was shot. On July 3, or Civic Day, veterans "reenacted" the Pickett-Pettigrew-Trimble Charge, but this time when they met at the Bloody Angle, they embraced each other and wept. The day closed, appropriately enough, with a grand fireworks display over Little Round Top. President Woodrow Wilson addressed a huge throng inside the Great Tent on National Day, July 4. At the closing ceremonies, all flags were lowered to half staff at noon in tribute to the dead of Gettysburg. Bands then played the National Anthem, the flags were raised to full staff, and the great reunion came to an end.

The U.S. Army Quartermaster Corps erected more than 6,500 tents to house approximately 57,200 people, including the returning veterans and the U.S. Army troops who supported the reunion. The tent city sprawled over 280 acres.

The crowd escaped the summer sun in the Great Tent near the Codori farm to hear
U.S. Secretary of War Lindley M. Garrison give his address on July 1, 1913.

The spirit of reunification was typified by these Confederate and Union veterans shaking hands.

On July 4, 1913, President Woodrow Wilson spoke in the Great Tent, addressing almost 15,000 people. He said, "We have found one another again as brothers and comrades in arms, enemies no longer, generous friends rather, our battles long past, the quarrel forgotten, except that we shall not forget the splendid valor, the manly devotion of the men arranged against one another, now grasping hands and smiling into each other's eyes."

Civilians who attended the reunion, such as this man talking with one of the Confederate veterans, found much to discuss with the old soldiers.

Pennsylvania Congressman
J. Hampton Moore addresses
the veterans at the Bloody
Angle on July 3, 1913.

U.S. Army cooks, such as these bakers, prepared 688,000 meals between June 29 and July 6, 1913—168,000 on July 4 alone. Meals were served in shifts, prepared in 173 kitchens by 2,000 cooks and helpers.

Veterans examine the statue of Major General Henry W. Slocum on July 1, 1913. Slocum, a New Yorker, commanded the Union XII Corps. His equestrian statue was erected on Stevens's Knoll in 1902.

As the veterans arrived for the reunion, they received programs and directions after they registered their names and regiments.

Union and Confederate veterans reminisce.

Veterans of the 111th New York Infantry view their regimental monument, with the Bryan house to their rear. The monument was dedicated on June 26, 1891.

"Mine had a ramrod," this Union veteran seems to be telling the young soldier as he examines the modern rifle.

The equestrian statue of Major General Oliver O. Howard, XI Corps commander, stands near the site of his headquarters on Cemetery Ridge. It was Howard, having directed much of the Union side of the battle on July 1, who selected the ridge as the Federal fallback position.

The veterans visited other parts of the encampment in between ceremonies and tours. These men are being welcomed to the state of Washington headquarters.

Veterans of Battery B, 1st New York Artillery, examine their monument and the cannons placed on the Emmitsburg Road facing the Codori farm.

Major General George Gordon Meade's equestrian statue was erected on Cemetery Ridge near the Bloody Angle in 1896. This photograph made at the 1913 reunion is titled "The Blue and The Gray viewing Pennsylvania's monument to George Gordon Meade."

The Pennsylvania State Monument, dedicated on September 27, 1910, is the most elaborate memorial on the field at Gettysburg. It holds the names of the more than 34,000 Pennsylvanians who fought there, as well as statues of Union generals George G. Meade, John F. Reynolds, Winfield S. Hancock, David B. Birney, Alfred Pleasonton, and David McM. Gregg. Alexander Curtin, the wartime governor of Pennsylvania, is also represented.

The photographers who covered the 1913 reunion often gave witty captions to their pictures. This one, showing two veterans playing cards near a cannon and piles of cannonballs, is entitled "Not so deadly a game, now."

Another clever caption, "Sighting over—50 years," was written for this photograph of two former Union artillerists behind a gun, with one sighting down the barrel.

Confederate veterans in a camp, with tents behind them, display their battle flags.

The headquarters of the Pennsylvania commission for the Fiftieth Anniversary Reunion stood on the grounds of Gettysburg College, June 25–July 10, 1913.

Following Spread: Confederate and Union veterans sit together on a fence to enjoy the festivities.

A Union veteran talks with a boy in this photograph captioned, "Telling it to his Grandson," taken on July 2, 1913.

Members of the Philadelphia Brigade Association and the Pickett's Division Association shake hands across the stone wall at the Bloody Angle, the "high-water mark," at 3:15 P.M., July 3, 1913.

Following Spread: Confederate and Union veterans sit atop the stone wall near the Bloody Angle.

167

Union and Confederate veterans pose beneath U.S. and Confederate flags, "Under Blue and Gray," at Gettysburg in July 1913.

Seventy-fifth Reunion

(1938)

By the time the seventy-fifth anniversary of the Battle of Gettysburg approached, few veterans survived, and the nation was not in much of a mood to commemorate a Civil War battle. The enormous bloodletting of World War I was a recent memory, war clouds were gathering again in Europe and in the Pacific, and the United States was struggling with limited success to emerge from the Great Depression. Pennsylvania formed another commission nonetheless, as did the federal government, but when the head of Pennsylvania's commission visited the annual conventions of the Grand Army of the Republic and the United Confederate Veterans in 1935, he met with stiff opposition. The commissioner, Paul Roy, persisted, however, and persuaded both groups to support the reunion.

Roy died a few months before the commemoration took place, but his hard work and powers of persuasion met with success. Once again, as in 1913, a tent city emerged outside Gettysburg to house the veterans, and once again large crowds attended the events. On opening day, June 29, there were 1,359 Union veterans and 486 Confederate veterans in the encampment. It was a sharp decline in numbers from 1913, but the population of Civil War veterans had been much reduced in the meantime. Most of those attending were more than ninety years of age.

To make the event easy on the old soldiers, each veteran was assigned a Boy Scout as an attendant, and most of the events were held nearby in Memorial Stadium on the campus of Gettysburg College. Welcoming speeches were given there on July 1, and on the second day a long parade passed through Gettysburg and ended in the stadium, where veterans of the country's later wars paid tribute to the old men. On July 3, a handful of survivors met again at the Bloody Angle to clasp hands across the stone wall, and that evening President Franklin D. Roosevelt unveiled the Eternal Light Peace Memorial on Oak Hill, which seventy-five years earlier had been a Confederate artillery position. The last day's events, on July 4, included reviews by the veterans in the stadium of passing cavalry, field and coast artillery, tanks, and infantry. An air show, with attack planes and B-17 bombers, must have caused a few of the Confederate veterans to wonder, "What if we had had a few of those?"

A retreat parade passed through the stadium late in the afternoon, followed by a formal guard-mount ceremony at the High Water Mark on Cemetery Ridge. A band concert and a searchlight display ended the day, and the reunion. The old men soon departed, leaving what Roosevelt called "a shrine to American patriotism"—Gettysburg National Military Park—to impart the memory of their sacrifices to succeeding generations.

This aerial view of the encampment constructed for the seventy-fifth anniversary commemoration was probably taken on June 25, 1938, before the official opening. The Union veterans' camp is at top-center and the Confederate camp at left-center.

Assembling the bed frames for the 1938 reunion was a massive task. By opening day—June 29—the camp population had reached 3,690, including veterans, their Boy Scout attendants, medical and kitchen personnel, police, and military personnel.

The tent city offered all the amenities of home, including haircuts.

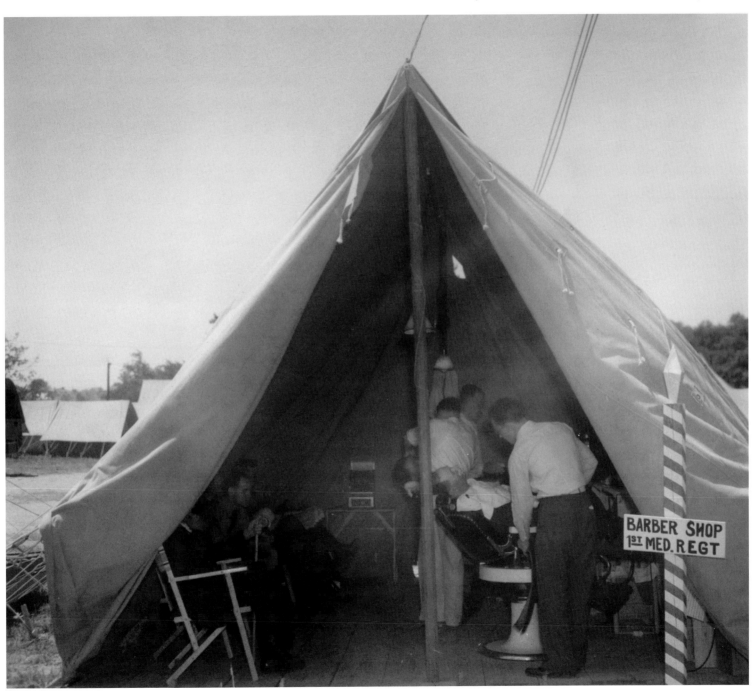

The thousands of volunteers who assisted at the reunion spent countless
hours working on such needed projects as painting signs.

The veterans, many of whom were in their nineties, received assistance from attendants throughout the reunion. The attendants' duties began at the train station, where many veterans arrived, as they escorted the old soldiers to their quarters in the tent city.

Vast crowds passed through Gettysburg National Military Park to the reunion, such as these people walking down the Emmitsburg Road. About 200,000 attended the dedication of the Eternal Light Peace Memorial on July 3.

Civilians who attended the reunion took opportunities to pose for photographs with the veterans.

U.S. Army troops drilled on the grounds of Gettysburg College, where many of the ceremonies and parades associated with the reunion were held. In the background is Stevens Hall, completed in 1868 and named for Senator Thaddeus Stevens, one of the college's founders.

Troops and vehicles pose in Memorial Stadium at Gettysburg College, the site of the parade and military exhibition on July 4, 1938.

Cavalrymen participated in the parades in Memorial Stadium during the reunion.

The spectators stand in Memorial Stadium during one of the ceremonies held there.

The returning veterans found an even more developed national park than they had seen in 1913. This aerial view shows the Soldiers' National Cemetery and Evergreen Cemetery.

By 1938, Gettysburg National Battlefield Park was well staffed. This undated photograph of park guards was probably taken a few years before the reunion.

The returning veterans saw familiar landmarks, such as the 91st Pennsylvania Infantry monument shown here, looking from the summit of Little Round Top toward Cemetery Hill. The monument was dedicated on September 12, 1889, and the photograph was taken about 1927.

Many iron interpretive markers were added to the park before 1912 to educate visitors about specific units and events. The marker and guns in this photograph stand where Captain Edward A. Marye's Battery, Fredericksburg Artillery, was positioned on Seminary Ridge after the first day's battle of July 1, 1863. Marye's Battery is credited with firing the first artillery shots of the battle on the Chambersburg Turnpike north of town before moving to the site shown here.

The Madison Light Artillery was a Louisiana unit assigned to Major General William Dorsey Pender's division. It was stationed on Seminary Ridge and supported both the Confederate attack at Sherfy's peach orchard on July 2, 1863, and the Pickett-Pettigrew-Trimble Charge the next day.

Captain James H. Cooper's Battery B, 1st Pennsylvania Light Artillery, was posted on East Cemetery Hill facing Confederate Major General Richard S. Ewell's corps on Benner's Hill. On July 2, 1863, Ewell launched a late-afternoon attack and the battery dueled successfully with the guns of Confederate Major Joseph W. Latimer's battalion. A monument to the battery was dedicated on September 11, 1889. The monument to the 4th Ohio Infantry is in the background.

Captain R. Bruce Rickett's Battery F, 1st Pennsylvania Light Artillery, occupied much the same ground on East Cemetery Hill as Cooper's Battery B on the afternoon of July 2, 1863. Battery F barely survived a charge by the Louisiana Tigers and held its position through the next day's fight.

For many years after the battle, there were no Confederate monuments at Gettysburg. The stringent rules that governed the placement of monuments, a lack of available funds in the Southern states, and the lack of interest in marking the scene of a notable defeat all played a role in keeping the field clear of Confederate memorials. Perhaps in part because of the spirit of reconciliation manifested at the 1913 reunion, on June 18, 1917, the Virginia monument was dedicated. The first monument for a Southern state, it features General Robert E. Lee and is located on Seminary Ridge. Other Southern monuments soon followed.

The Alabama State Monument was erected in 1933. It stands close to the Emmitsburg Road, near the position on the Confederate right flank from which Brigadier General Evander K. Law's Alabama brigade launched its attack on Little Round Top on July 2, 1863.

President Franklin D. Roosevelt arrived at the train station about six o'clock on the evening of July 3 to unveil the Eternal Light Peace Memorial. This photograph shows him in his car with Secret Service men just after he detrained.

A veteran took the opportunity to speak with President Franklin D. Roosevelt before the motorcade to the Peace Memorial got underway.

At the Peace Memorial ceremony, President Franklin D. Roosevelt addressed the huge crowd and honored the veterans in attendance. "Men who wore the blue and men who wore the gray are here together," he said, "a fragment spared by time. They are brought here by the memories of old divided loyalties, but they meet here in united loyalty to a united cause which the unfolding years have made it easier to see. All of them we honor, not asking under which flag they fought then—thankful that they stand together under one flag now."

President Franklin D. Roosevelt (center) and other dignitaries viewed the scene at the Peace Memorial from the speakers' platform.

This snapshot was taken standing among the crowd shortly before the
Peace Memorial was unveiled.

The Eternal Light Peace Memorial was intended both as a tribute to the soldiers who fought at Gettysburg and as a symbol of eternal peace in the United States. President Franklin D. Roosevelt, in his speech at the unveiling ceremony, declared, "On behalf of the people of the United States, I accept this monument in the spirit of brotherhood and peace." Roosevelt also said, "Immortal deeds and immortal words have created here at Gettysburg a shrine to American patriotism." Indeed, no other hallowed ground in America stirs such emotions, even today, as Gettysburg National Battlefield Park.

Notes on the Photographs

These notes, listed by page number, attempt to include all aspects known of the photographs. Each of the photographs is identified by the page number, photograph's title or description, photographer and collection, archive, and call or box number when applicable. Although every attempt was made to collect all available data, in some cases complete data was unavailable due to the age and condition of some of the photographs and records.

II   **GETTYSBURG MAP**
Library of Congress
3g01825u

VI   **STATE MONUMENT**
Pennsylvania State Archives
m218-Box28-Folder2

X   **SEMINARY RIDGE VIEW**
U.S. Army Military Institute
SC206-RG667S-VOL.19-P.917

3   **LEE HEADQUARTERS**
The Library of Congress
lc-b811-2395

4   **MEADE HEADQUARTERS**
The Library of Congress
lc-b811-259

5   **McPHERSON FARM**
U.S. Army Military Institute
00887u

6   **McPHERSON'S WOODS**
Gettysburg National Military
Park Library
2b2001

7   **STEVENS KNOLL**
The Library of Congress
cwpb 03772

8   **LITTLE ROUND TOP**
The Library of Congress
lc-b811-2384

9   **DEVIL'S DEN**
The Library of Congress
lc-b811-2399

10   **LITTLE ROUND TOP**
The Library of Congress
lc-b817-7493

12   **CULP'S HILL**
The Library of Congress
lc-b811-2390

13   **BATTLEFIELD ARTIST**
The Library of Congress
cwpb 00074

14   **GETTYSBURG SKETCH**
The Library of Congress
3g03260u

16   **BREASTWORKS**
The Library of Congress
lc-b811-2387

17   **BATTERY 1**
U.S. Army Military Institute
SC206-RG490S-VOL 2,P.263

18   **CONFEDERATE PRISONERS**
The Library of Congress
lc-b811-2288

19   **SHARPSHOOTER'S HOME**
The Library of Congress
cwpb 00069

20   **WHITE'S STONE HOUSE**
The Library of Congress
cwp 4a40114

21   **BRYAN HOUSE**
U.S. Army Military Institute
SC206-RG98S-65.20, BRYAN

22   **LUTHERAN SEMINARY**
The Library of Congress
lc-b811-2393

24   **SHARPSHOOTING COVER**
The Library of Congress
cwpb 01635

25   **TANEY FARMHOUSE**
U.S. Army Military Institute
01636u

26   **LITTLE ROUND TOP**
The Library of Congress
lc-b811-2400

27   **ROSE FARM**
U.S. Army Military Institute
SC206-RG667S-VOL.29,P.1406

28   **BALTIMORE TURNPIKE**
National Archives
165-sb-035

29   **UNION DEAD**
National Archives
165-sb-036

30   **CONFEDERATE DEAD**
The Library of Congress
cwpb 00908

32   **ROSE FARM DEAD**
The Library of Congress
cph 01828

33   **DEVIL'S DEN DEAD**
The Library of Congress
lc-b811-277

34   **SHARPSHOOTER DEAD**
The Library of Congress
ppmsc 00171

36   **DEVIL'S DEN**
U.S. Army Military Institute
SC206-RG98S-4.8

37 SLAUGHTER PEN
The Library of Congress
cwpb 00895

38 CONFEDERATE GRAVES
The Library of Congress
cwpb 00843

39 TROSTLE FARM
The Library of Congress
lot 4168

40 BY THE SLAUGHTER PEN
The Library of Congress
cwpb 00880

41 GEORGIAN IN ROSE WOODS
The Library of Congress
cph 3g01830

42 UNFIT FOR SERVICE
The Library of Congress
cph 3g01829

43 POSED DEAD SOLDIERS
U.S. Army Military Institute
SC206-RG98S-4.5

44 EVERGREEN CEMETERY
National Archives
165-sb-039.tif

45 AMPUTATION
National Archives
079-t-2265

46 NATIONAL CEMETERY
National Archives
111-b-0357

47 EASTERN CEMETERY HILL
National Archives
200s-pierc-m276-276-2

48 JOHN L. BURNS
The Library of Congress
cwpb 01660

50 SANITARY COMMISSION
The Library of Congress
lc-b811-238

51 TENT HOSPITALS
U.S. Army Military Institute
SC206-RG490S-VOL 7,P.300-3

52 CAMP LETTERMAN
U.S. Army Military Institute
SC206-RG667S-
VOL.82,P.4125

53 HOSPITAL KITCHEN
U.S. Army Military Institute
SC206-RG667S-VOL.82,P.
L412

54 SANITARY COMMISSION
U.S. Army Military Institute
SC206-RG667S-
VOL.82,P.4126

56 DEDICATION CEREMONY
The Library of Congress
cwpb 00673

57 SOLDIER'S MONUMENT
U.S. Army Military Institute
SC206-RG667S-
VOL.87,P.4370

58 SUPPLIES FOR SOLDIERS
The Library of Congress
cwpb 03913

60 SOLDIER'S NATIONAL
CEMETERY
The Library of Congress
cwpb 03922

62 STACKED GUNS
The Library of Congress
cwpb 03744

64 HOFF'S CLERK
The Library of Congress
cwpb 03998

65 CAPTAIN HOFF
The Library of Congress
cph 3c06651

66 50TH INFANTRY
The Library of Congress
cwpb 03722

67 SMYSER MONUMENT
U.S. Army Military Institute
SC206-RG667S-
VOL.87,P.4360

68 TELFORD SOLDIERS
The Library of Congress
cwpb 03896

70 50TH PENNSYLVANIA
INFANTRY
The Library of Congress
cwpb 03652

72 COLONEL DAVIS
The Library of Congress
cwpb 03935

74 GRAVE MARKER
U.S. Army Military Institute
SC206-RG667S-
VOL.87,P.4360

75 ROCK CREEK
The Library of Congress
cph 3c17670

76 SPANGLER'S MEADOW
The Library of Congress
lot 4167

77 GETTYSBURG VIEW
The Library of Congress
lot 11957-4

78 ORPHAN'S HOMESTEAD
Gettysburg National Military
Park Library
24S-1069

79 LUTHERAN SEMINARY
The Library of Congress
3c17885u

80 CULP'S HILL POSE
The Library of Congress
cph 3c12580

81 BATTLEFIELD OBSERVATORY
The Library of Congress
cph 3b11174

82 1878 REUNION
U.S. Army Military Institute
SC206-RG98S-27.83, G.A.R.

83 REENACTMENTS
U.S. Army Military Institute
SC206-RG98S-27.84, G.A.R.

84 CODORI FARM
U.S. Army Military Institute
SC206-RG667S-VOL.28,P.L137

85 GREGG CALVARY SHAFT
U.S. Army Military Institute
SC206-RG667S-
VOL.70,P.3463

86 WEED MONUMENT
U.S. Army Military Institute
SC206-RG667S-
VOL.48,P.2427

87 LITTLE ROUND TOP
U.S. Army Military Institute
SC206-RG667S-
VOL.65,P.3247

88 VIEW FROM LITTLE ROUND
TOP
U.S. Army Military Institute
SC206-RG667S-
VOL.75,P.3736

89 PICKETT'S CHARGE
U.S. Army Military Institute
SC206-RG667S-VOL.48,P.2426

90 CEMETERY RIDGE
U.S. Army Military Institute
SC206-RG667S-VOL.38,P.1876

91 JENNIE WADE
U.S. Army Military Institute
SC206-RG667S-VOL.38,P.L187

92 2ND INFANTRY POSING
U.S. Army Military Institute
SC206-RG667S-VOL.6,P.283,D

93 96TH INFANTRY
U.S. Army Military Institute
SC206-RG98S-27.12,VETS

94 151ST REGIMENT
U.S. Army Military Institute
SC206-RG98S-41.104, 151ST

95 9TH BATTERY MONUMENT
U.S. Army Military Institute
SC206-RG667S-VOL.91,P.4691

96 UNION BREASTWORKS
U.S. Army Military Institute
SC206-RG667S-VOL.75,P.3733

97 12TH INFANTRY MONUMENT
U.S. Army Military Institute
SC206-RG667S-VOL.75,P.L373

98 BUGLER
U.S. Army Military Institute
SC206-RG667S-VOL.111,P.L57

99 LADIES POSE WITH CANNON
U.S. Army Military Institute
SC206-RG667S-VOL.111,P.570

100 VETERANS POSE
U.S. Army Military Institute
SC206-RG667S-VOL.70,P.3464

101 KNAP'S BATTERY
U.S. Army Military Institute
SC206-RG667S-VOL.65,P.3246

102 GETTYSBURG COLLEGE
U.S. Army Military Institute
SC206-RG667S-VOL.19,P.927

103 REYNOLDS MONUMENT
U.S. Army Military Institute
SC206-RG667S-VOL6,P.L281,J

104 SPANGLER'S SPRING
U.S. Army Military Institute
SC206-RG667S-VOL.28,P.L137

105 VISITOR TO DEVIL'S DEN
U.S. Army Military Institute
SC206-RG98S-27.77

106 DEVIL'S DEN VETERANS
U.S. Army Military Institute
SC206-RG26S-.28

107 MAJOR GENERAL SICKLES
U.S. Army Military Institute
SC206-RG26S-.28

108 WARREN STATUE
U.S. Army Military Institute
SC206-RG113S-.584

109 HANCOCK STATUE
U.S. Army Military Institute
SC206-RG98S-1.74

110 155TH INFANTRY STATUE
U.S. Army Military Institute
SC206-RG98S-1.75

111 68TH INFANTRY MEMORIAL
U.S. Army Military Institute
SC206-RG667S-VOL.87,P.4354

112 EVERGREEN CEMETERY
U.S. Army Military Institute
SC206-RG667S-VOL.87,P.4360

113 ZOOK MEMORIAL
U.S. Army Military Institute
SC206-RG667S-VOL.87,P.4360

114 SOLDIER'S NATIONAL CEMETERY
U.S. Army Military Institute
SC206-RG98S-7.194

115 ROUND TOPS
U.S. Army Military Institute
SC206-RG667S-VOL.28,P.L136

116 NATIONAL CEMETERY
The Library of Congress
cph 3b36744

117 SPANGLER'S SPRING
The Library of Congress
cph 3c00945

118 CLASS OF 1903
Gettysburg National Military
Park Library
29V-1103

120 DEVIL'S DEN
The Library of Congress
6a09475u

121 PRESIDENT TAFT
Gettysburg National Military
Park Library
SF-5E-026

122 TAFT BY MEMORIAL
Gettysburg National Military
Park Library
20P-2010

123 MILITARY ENCAMPMENT
U.S. Army Military Institute
SC206-RG100S-S

124 GETTYSBURG
The Library of Congress
pan 6a9486

125 MEADE PANORAMA
The Library of Congress
pan 6a9492

126 BARLOW'S KNOLL
The Library of Congress
ggbain 13855

128 1ST INFANTRY MONUMENT
U.S. Army Military Institute
SC206-RG667SVOL.87,P.4354

129 CHAMBERSBURG TURNPIKE
The Library of Congress
pan 6a09480

130 MONUMENTAL CHANGES
The Library of Congress
pan 6a09510

133 REUNION TENTS
The Library of Congress
pan 6a31636

134 GREAT TENT
The Library of Congress
lc-usz62-107567

135 SHAKING HANDS
The Library of Congress
cph 3b34842

136 PRESIDENT WILSON
The Library of Congress
ggbain 13861

137 CIVILIANS AND SOLDIERS
U.S. Army Military Institute
SC206-RG100S

138 BLOODY ANGLE
The Library of Congress
ggbain 13508

140 U.S. ARMY COOKS
The Library of Congress
cph 3b39601

141 SLOCUM STATUE
Pennsylvania State Archives
r025#024-Vol4p219

142 **VETERANS ARRIVE AT REUNION**
Pennsylvania State Archives
r025#024-Vol4p207

144 **VETERANS REMINISCE**
Pennsylvania State Archives
r025#024-Vol4p215

146 **11TH INFANTRY MONUMENT**
Pennsylvania State Archives
r025#024-Vol4p209

148 **OLD AND NEW**
Pennsylvania State Archives
r025#024-Vol4p203

149 **VETERANS GREET**
Pennsylvania State Archives
r025#024-Vol4p201

150 **HOWARD STATUE**
Pennsylvania State Archives
m218-Box28-Folder2

151 **WASHINGTON HQ**
Pennsylvania State Archives
r025#024-Vol4p193

152 **BATTERY B MONUMENT**
Pennsylvania State Archives
r025#024-Vol4p199

154 **MEADE STATUE**
Pennsylvania State Archives
r025#024-Vol4p179

156 **UNION VETERAN**
Pennsylvania State Archives
r025#024-Vol4p177

157 **SONS AND GRANDSONS**
Pennsylvania State Archives
r025#024-Vol4p175

158 **GRANDDAUGHTERS**
Pennsylvania State Archives
r025#024-Vol4p173

159 **PENNSYLVANIA STATE MONUMENT**
Pennsylvania State Archives
m218-Box28-Folder2

160 **NOT SO DEADLY A GAME**
Pennsylvania State Archives
r025#024-Vol4p249

161 **SIGHTING OVER 50 YEARS**
Pennsylvania State Archives
r025#024-Vol4p247

162 **CONFEDERATE VETERANS**
Pennsylvania State Archives
r025#024-Vol4p243

163 **PENNSYLVANIA COMMISSION**
Pennsylvania State Archives
r025#024-Vol4p235

164 **VETERANS SIT TOGETHER**
Pennsylvania State Archives
r025#024-Vol4p241

166 **GENERATIONS**
Pennsylvania State Archives
r025#024-Vol4p249

167 **HANDSHAKE AT THE BLOODY ANGLE**
Pennsylvania State Archives
r025-50thAnnyGettysburg

168 **VETERANS ON STONE WALL**
Pennsylvania State Archives
r025#024-Vol4p243

170 **BLUE AND GRAY**
The Library of Congress
ggbain 13841

173 **AERIAL VIEW**
Pennsylvania State Archives
m281-Box01-Folder

174 **ASSEMBLING BEDFRAMES**
U.S. Army Military Institute
SC206-RG834S-SC #109085

175 **HAIRCUTS IN TENT CITY**
U.S. Army Military Institute
SC206-RG834S-SC #109277, 7

176 **PAINTING SIGNS**
U.S. Army Military Institute
SC206-RG393S-1938

177 **VETERAN'S ATTENDANTS**
U.S. Army Military Institute
SC206-RG393S-1938

178 **CROWDS AT REUNION**
U.S. Army Military Institute
SC206-RG393S-1938

179 **CIVILIANS POSE**
U.S. Army Military Institute
SC206-RG393S-1938

180 **GETTYSBURG COLLEGE**
U.S. Army Military Institute
SC206-RG834S-SC #109162

181 **MEMORIAL STADIUM**
U.S. Army Military Institute
SC206-RG393S-1938

182 **CALVARY PARADES**
U.S. Army Military Institute
SC206-RG393S-1938,109263

183 **SPECTATORS**
U.S. Army Military Institute
SC206-RG393S-1938

184 **NATIONAL PARK**
Pennsylvania State Archives
m281-Box01-Folder45

186 **PARK GUARDS**
U.S. Army Military Institute
SC206-RG112S-4.51

187 **91ST INFANTRY MONUMENT**
The Library of Congress
cph 3c01062

188 **MARYE'S BATTERY**
U.S. Army Military Institute
SC206-RG112S-4.29

189 **MADISON LIGHT ARTILLERY**
U.S. Army Military Institute
SC206-RG112S-4.38

190 **BATTERY B**
U.S. Army Military Institute
SC206-RG112S-3.92

191 **RICKETT'S BATTERY**
U.S. Army Military Institute
SC206-RG112S-3.108

192 **SEMINARY RIDGE**
Pennsylvania State Archives
m218-Box28-Folder2

193 **ALABAMA STATE MONUMENT**
Pennsylvania State Archives
m218-Box28-Folder2]

194 **ROOSEVELT**
U.S. Army Military Institute
SC206-RG393S-1938

195 **VETERAN AND ROOSEVELT**
U.S. Army Military Institute
SC206-RG393S-1938

196 **PEACE MEMORIAL CEREMONY**
U.S. Army Military Institute
SC206-RG393S-1938

197 **SPEAKERS' PLATFORM**
U.S. Army Military Institute
SC206-RG393S-1938

198 **PEACE MEMORIAL CROWD**
Gettysburg National Military
Park Library
SF-5E-1956

199 **ETERNAL LIGHT PEACE MEMORIAL**
Pennsylvania State Archives
m213-CountyFile-Box01

206 **GETTYSBURG ADDRESS**
Library of Congress